Lisa —

Can't wait for you to see how
simple & powerful this customer
experience program has been — I
think it will change the way we
all behave in a UBER-AMAZON
economy —

Cheers,

Cross Hoffer

NO MORE CUSTOMER FRICTION

First printed by:
LSC Communications Book Group
4101 Winfield Road
Warrenville, IL 60555

Contact Ross Shafer: www.RossShafer.com

ISBN: 9780692860632

Printed in the United States of America

Cover and text design by theBookDesigners

A BOLD BLUEPRINT FOR RAISING CUSTOMER SCORES

NO MORE CUSTOMER FRICTION

ROSS SHAFER

DEDICATION

I want to dedicate this book to my wife, Leah Shafer. She is a professional singer who has entertained millions in professional sports stadiums and countless church concert venues.

Her high profile has brought quite a degree of fame; which has (subsequently) awarded her with faster service at restaurants. She is often escorted to escape long lines.

And, when call center people learn who she is, her service issues are solved almost instantly. She knows this treatment isn't "fair" but admits that "celebrities" invariably experience less friction in life.

However, because she has a servant's heart, Leah has woven those experiences into her own esthetician business (www.SkinByLeah.com).

She credits her success to the attitude, *"Everybody should be treated like a celebrity. Make a person feel extraordinary and you'll have a customer for life."*

TABLE OF CONTENTS

THE SHORTEST INTRODUCTON YOU'LL EVER READ

I developed this step-by-step blueprint for clients who wanted to raise their customer satisfaction, effort, customer engagement, and customer experience scores. My system is reliable, simple, refined, and (when applied) works every time.

1) You will learn specific behaviors that dramatically reduce (or eliminate) your customer complaints.

2) You will learn how to repair customer relationships that are "at risk" due to your past missteps.

3) And, you'll learn how to erase the friction from all of your processes; which results in growing long-term customers.

I'm ready when you are.

—Ross Shafer

CHAPTER 1

SCORES ONLY GO UP WHEN YOU START WITH A BASELINE

WE SCORE EVERYTHING THAT MATTERS

As insecure teenagers, we obsessed over how our boyfriend or girlfriend felt about us. As adults, we still wonder if people like us. Many men and women rate the looks of another person with a score of 1-10.

Millions of people wager money on the outcome of a sporting event.

At work, our annual bonus is scored by how much we sell - or by how much money we save the company.

And of course we ask our customers to give us feedback on our performance. We change our pricing, our array of products and services to suit our customer's shifting needs. The best of us change our behaviors based upon those customer comments. And, if there are no customers to ask, we hire secret shoppers to spy on our employees.

Even though customer-centric companies seemed to marshal more growth, many leaders were still reluctant to draw a cause-and-effect between better service and higher revenue.

That is, until two brilliant thought leaders offered tangible proof.

Writer and consultant Jeanne Bliss, author of "Chief Customer Officer" and "I Love You More Than My Dog," has convinced thousands of companies to make room at the C-suite table for a customer service advocate. Researcher Fred Reichheld, author of "The Ultimate Question," introduced a revolutionary customer service evaluation system that proved customer satisfaction was indeed a growth engine. His disciples include the globe's largest companies.

Forrester (yes, *that* research firm) suggests that a $1 billion company (i.e., Cheesecake Factory, Old Dominion Trucking, and Public Storage) would experience a $100 million boost in revenue from a ten percent improvement in their customer experience scores. The dots between happy customers and higher revenue have been inextricably connected.

ELIMINATING CUSTOMER
FRICTION CAN SAVE A COMPANY

You just have to eliminate the complaints.

Eliminate all customer friction and make it easy for people to buy from you.

Below are three case studies from companies that simply eliminated customer complaints.

> **Comcast** (the largest cable and broadcast provider in the U.S.) knew they had to reverse their miserable customer care ratings. So, they added service techs and billing efficiencies to speed up response times by 18 percent. Comcast took great pains to eliminate the common complaints. For the first time in eight years, they added 1.4 million new Internet customers and profits grew more than two percent to $1.97 billion.

> **Lego**, the interlocking brick toy maker, was on the verge of bankruptcy. They were getting complaints that their toy designs were getting stale. In some cases, the toys had to be sold below cost. So Lego hired die-hard fans of the brand to create new and exciting products. Lego also tied into movie franchises like Star Wars and Batman. By listening to their customers Lego reversed a dangerous slide. Today, Lego is the largest toy company in the world.

LEADING ENERGY COMPANY

The customer scores of a **leading energy company** languished in last place until I introduced my "No More Customer Friction" method to them. Through 22 training sessions in 10 cities, we increased their J.D. Power customer scores by 21 points--catapulting them into first place.

WHICH SCORING SYSTEM IS BEST?

For this to work, you must start with a baseline score. So, the best scoring system is the one you already own.

Don't change it yet.

You know how your system works, so you'll know when your scores go up. That's our primary goal here...GET THOSE CUSTOMER SCORES UP! If your company doesn't use a customer scoring system yet, check out NPS, CSAT, CES, or Magnet Recognition (which is hospital specific) *detailed in the appendix of this book.*

You're welcome.

TIME AND FRICTION ARE THE ROOT CAUSES FOR SINKING SCORES

Customers never have enough time to complete their daily to-do lists. When a customer runs out of time (before completing their self-inflicted schedule), they lose their minds. They get edgy, angry and disagreeable. Our job is to

SAVE TIME for our customers. They should be able to buy from us, order from us, talk to us, or deal with a problem without any CUSTOMER FRICTION (this is a word sign you should erect in your office). Customer Friction is anything that disrupts a customer's expectation of the time it takes to buy from you — or deal with a problem. We all need to stop making mistakes that steal time from our customers. Our scores will drop if we:

- Commit dumb blunders
- Show rude behavior
- Neglect customer requests
- Get caught being incompetent
- Make people wait
- Forget a promise we made to a customer.

CONVENIENCE EASES THE TENSION OF REAL LIFE

Jeannie Walters wants every vendor to consider how your products and services intersect with the customer's real life. Walters is the Chief Customer Experience Investigator and founder of 360Connext, a global consulting firm specializing in the cornerstones of customer experience: customer engagement, and employee engagement. Walters emphasizes that mobile is an undeniable purchasing force in that people are spending 200+ hours a year in transit. For example, the convenience of using your smart device to buy groceries on the train, during your commute, could far outweigh the otherwise convenient experience of getting your groceries delivered to your home.

MORE CONVENIENCE, SAVING TIME, & ELIMINATING CUSTOMER FRICTION are the core principles of this book. Here are three companies that have elevated these concepts to epic levels.

JUST WALK OUT

Presently, Amazon has opened their first Amazon Go grocery store in Seattle, WA. As you know, Amazon's brand grew on the premise of flawless customer service. Now they have enhanced their brand goal to be friction-free. Type AMAZON GO into any search engine and watch their video.

The cost and SKU of every grocery item in the 1,800 square foot store is linked to your Amazon account. You walk in, and start taking food off the shelves. The app "senses" when you have added an item to your virtual cart. If you decide to put something back, the app automatically takes that item off your bill. There are no lines and no waiting. Amazon calls it "Just Walk Out Technology." Since the app automatically tabulates everything, Amazon Go has also eliminated shoplifting.

PICK ME UP RIGHT NOW

Uber has revolutionized convenient transportation. It's as easy as downloading their mobile app. Enter your credit card number in the app. Order a car to pick you up and the app's mapping system tells the driver where you are. The app tells you when to expect the car, how much the trip will cost you, the driver's name, the make and license number of the vehicle. After your ride, you get out and walk away. No tip to give the driver as it is baked into the price of the ride.

THE DOCTOR WILL SKYPE YOU NOW

Instead of making a traditional doctor's appointment, Doctors on Demand and AnywhereCare offer one-on-one video conferencing either over your smartphone or your laptop. Yes, you can get medical advice without having to visit the doctor's office. Pat Basu is the chief medical officer for Doctors on Demand. He says, "Two of the most important skills we have as physicians are looking and listening. Video conferencing lets me use those skills and diagnose colds, coughs, and even sprains in a manner more convenient for you." What a brilliant way to reduce the friction of visiting the doctor...and saving a patient's time.

Some of you may be thinking, "Yeah, but we WOW our customers all the time. Isn't that enough?"

In the next chapter I hope to convince you that WOWs alone will not raise your scores as high as you'd like.

CHAPTER 2

THE DIFFERENCE BETWEEN WOW & POW

PRECISE LANGUAGE
PREDICTS BETTER BEHAVIOR

Once customer care was linked to profits, the customer service training landscape became cluttered with new monikers like Wowing the customer, customer experience, customer connection, customer expectations, customer empathy, customer engagement, customer-centric, voice-of-the-customer, and others.

The aforementioned are all fine terms but, in my opinion, we should further simplify the language.

We all know the word WOW describes a positive customer experience. From now on let's use the word POW to describe a poor customer experience outcome. Less POWs result in less *Customer Complaints*.

YOU DON'T HAVE TO WOW PEOPLE

The overwhelming majority of today's leaders were taught to "exceed customer expectations" - to "WOW" the customer.

For the uninitiated, a WOW is the unexpected delight that surprises the customer and differentiates us from our competition. A perfectly executed WOW is designed to make such a lasting impression on the customer that our efforts live on as a glorious story the customer can tell their friends. Unfortunately, our predictions are often just that. We often find out that WOW-ing the customer doesn't generate the flood of happy customers we had hoped.

Leaders are often perplexed and disappointed when they learn that WOWs aren't the loyalty formula they presumed. When they dig into the customer data they find that only a small number of customers returned because the company over-delivered on the brand promise. Worse, their market share takes a big dip when a far larger number of customers bolt to a competitor simply due to bad service.

INSTEAD, EMBRACE THE POW

Indulge me for a moment.

Let's put the WOWS on hold and redirect our focus to the POWS. When we do or say something that incites a customer to get angry, complain, or leave... I define those disappointments as POW moments. POWS are like a punch in the customer's gut. POWS can result in lost revenue. POWS waste a customer's time and energy. POWS can lead to a viral boycott of your goods and services. POWS can derail your customer's day, tarnish your brand, and eradicate you from being a customer's first choice. POWS can be so devastating that, from our research, ONE POW can erase FIVE WOWS.

At its core, a POW moment infects a transaction with unnecessary inconvenience and friction. However, if we eliminate the POWS we can handily capture more loyalty than a bucket of WOWS.

WHY SPEND THE WRONG MONEY ON YOUR CUSTOMERS?

Let's be logical about the time and money you spend in your attempt to WOW the customer.

How much cash do you waste to surprise the customer, offer giveaways, hand out free products, succumb to double refunds, or throw in free shipping?

It's very costly to buy a customer's love with perks; especially when the volume of return customers is much higher when you spend money on empowered training, meeting the customer's needs, and smoothing out your transactional processes.

Customers will reward you with loyalty if you just reduce the effort it takes for them to do business with you.

Loyalty favors the company that can help customers solve their problems faster and easier.

But don't take my word for it. Here's what two of the leading customer measurement companies have to say.

> At CSAT (Customer SATisfaction) we talk to the customer to determine what they want and how they want us to deliver. Under-promise, don't over-deliver (it's better to meet, not necessarily exceed, their expectations rather than fail or disappoint them).
>
> CES (Customer Effort Score) research showed that, "Service organizations create loyal customers primarily by reducing customer effort – i.e. helping them solve their problems quickly and easily – not by delighting them in service interactions."

POW MOMENT TRIGGERS

The customer hears you say, "There is nothing else I can do."

You tell a customer you cannot help them because, "It's not our policy."

The item a customer ordered is not in stock (even though you said it was).

You won't take responsibility for your mistake.

You ignore, neglect, or forget an important customer request.

DURING EVERY TRANSACTION...

We should ask ourselves,

"Am I saying or doing anything that will result in a POW moment for this customer?

"Will the customer lose more time in their day from what I'm doing?"

"Will this customer say I have added more friction to the transaction?"

Your culture can become customer-centric if you are hyper-aware of these words and phrases.

RESPECT <u>TIME</u>. <u>CUSTOMER</u> <u>FRICTION</u>. <u>WOW</u>. <u>POW</u>.

What kinds of POW moments make customers score you lower? You are about to find out.

CHAPTER 3

KNOW WHAT CUSTOMERS CONSIDER POW MOMENTS

TRANSACTIONAL FRICTION HAS MANY SUBCATEGORIES

Friction is the problem. But to correct it in all forms we have to listen to what customers consider the root cause. Not delivering on your brand promise is friction because a disappointed customer now feels like they were tricked and must spend time researching an alternative product or service. Incompetence is friction because the customer has to spend extra time explaining their problem to multiple people to find a solution. Ignoring the customer is friction because the rest of their daily schedule has been interrupted.

I have read thousands of frustrating customer experience letters and blogs from around the world. Regardless of geography, the results proved that human beings are prone to common emotional reactions when experiencing similar patterns of mistreatment. I first published these findings in my book "The Customer Shouts Back" and have updated them for this book. You may want to hide your eyes.

34% OF CUSTOMERS FELT CHEATED AND/OR BETRAYED BY YOUR BRAND PROMISE

Your marketing efforts attracted a customer who was thrilled to find you. But when they perceived that your promise fell short, these customers felt cheated. If the customer didn't get a refund, a credit, or an apology, their angry reaction often set off a social media firestorm. These customers couldn't wait to lash out at the company.

> I have a rule. Screw me once and I might forgive you. Bone me twice and you better walk on the other side of the street.

> I don't have time for swindlers and snake oil folks. But I'll take the time to eliminate these ******* from ever cheating anybody else.

> I've had it with everyone in your company. I hope you all die in a forklift accident.

23% OF CUSTOMERS SAID THE COMPANY BLAMED THEM FOR THE PROBLEM

A staggering number of companies don't take responsibility for problems. Complainers stated that employees made no effort to be responsible or solve the problem themselves. Instead, they deferred the problem to a "superior" or "manager." In some cases the employee recited, "It's not our policy" or "It's not my department." I heard many complaints where the company told customers, "There is nothing wrong with our product. You just don't know how to use it."

> **Example:** I bought a counter depth refrigerator 18 months ago. The freezer freezes everything except the ice cream; which never gets hard. I can easily dish it out with a spoon. The first repairman said it was plenty cold enough, even when I showed him the soft ice cream. It doesn't even get cold enough to chill my milk. The second repairman told me to keep milk in the very back where the cold comes out. Is he kidding me? Where in the manual does it say to keep milk in the back?

18% OF CUSTOMERS FELT IGNORED.

Customers interpret "being ignored" as when a company employee is too engaged in a personal phone call to notice the customer, or doing busy work like inventory or finishing up a previous transaction, or putting a telephone customer on hold and never coming back on the line. Others felt that if they filled out an online customer service form...that it got vaporized somewhere in cyberspace. They hate having to repeat their personal information every time they were transferred to a new person.

> I was standing directly in front of the clerk holding my receipt but she not only ignored me - she kept talking to her friend. I said, "Excuse me, I'd like to..." and she turned away laughing with her friend as they walked to another aisle. I'll never go back.

> I filled out the online form to register my complaint but I ran out of characters before I could explain everything. When I pushed the "submit" button, I wondered if my letter even went to anybody. It's been over three months and I've never received a response.

10% SAID THEY HAD
TO DEAL WITH INCOMPETENCE

Customers repeatedly said, "They can't even get the basics right." What does that mean? Getting the basics wrong refers to such errors as not returning a phone call, not answering an email, not delivering products that were broken, parts missing from the order, inadequate tech support, and misplacing a customer's extended warranty.

The following conversation is an example of incompetence in the business-to-business sector:

> BUYER: I want to place an order for your BVX cloud services.
>
> CALL CENTER: Everybody is out of the office right now.
>
> BUYER: Are you familiar with the BVX bundle?
>
> CALL CENTER: (pause) I'm not sure...I need to put you on hold.
>
> (Three minutes later)
>
> CALL CENTER: Can you tell me what price you were quoted?
>
> BUYER: I'm with The (XXXX) Company. I'm a Platinum Class vendor. Just look up my account number?
>
> CALL CENTER: (pause) I don't think I have access to those accounts.
>
> BUYER: Just stop! Have my sales rep call me.
>
> CALL CENTER: Who is your rep?
>
> BUYER: &%$#!* (CLICK!)

8% WERE TREATED RUDELY

Customers blew the rudeness whistle on employees, managers, supervisors, and even senior level partners. Yikes! Customers described rudeness as, "totally dismissive of my concerns," or "they were condescending toward me."

To me, the crime-of-all-time was, "He got in my face and called me an idiot."

(Even if the customer is a complete idiot, it's not a wise move to call them that.)

> I went to a large home improvement store to buy some new patio furniture. When I got there I saw what I wanted, but I couldn't find anyone to sell it to me. I thought, "Maybe I'm supposed to serve myself." I went outside to see if I could find a big flat cart. No luck. So I asked this young employee if he could find a flat cart for me. He said, "You'll have to look in the parking lot." I told him I was just out there. He looked at me and said, "Well if I go out there it'll be the same as you looking. I can't do any better than that." I left fuming and bought my furniture somewhere else.

7% OF CUSTOMERS ARE UNHAPPY WITH ANYTHING YOU DO

You can't please everybody. As you will read in Chapter Five, some customers are so personally unstable that you will never understand their motives or their complaints. But you must try to soothe them because you don't know how vast their social reach may be. Even "crazy" people have an audience.

NO ACTION IS TOO SMALL

Customers will also "shut their wallets" when you say or do something very small. Even inconsequential POW behavior can drive them away.

When you don't smile at a customer, they feel disliked.

If you don't make eye contact, they feel unimportant.

When you don't acknowledge the customer, either on the phone, through email, or in person, they feel rejected.

If the customer overhears you use foul language they feel embarrassed, insulted, or angry.

IS THERE A SPECIFIC DEMOGRAPHIC THAT COMPLAINED MORE THAN OTHERS?

In addition to making sure you never commit the sins listed above, you should pay special attention to the most prolific complainers. Ready to know who they are? Hold your breath and turn the page.

CHAPTER 4

HEED THE NEEDS OF EPIC COMPLAINERS

WOMEN ARE EPIC

Considering that 84 percent of *all* consumer purchasing is accomplished by women, is it not then a mathematical parallel that a similar percentage of women complain about their poor service experiences? Another staggering statistic is that women over 50 years old control ¾ of all the financial wealth in the United States. Due to genetics, occupational choices, and certain cultural mores, men die earlier.

Therefore, it shouldn't surprise you that:

Women buy more.
Women save more.
Women budget more.
Women also buy on behalf of their parents and friends.
Women tend to have higher expectations for customer service.
Women tend to build closer relationships with their preferred brands and are eager to tell their friends about their purchases.

Women buy more frequently than men.

Women connect to advertisements and brands through social media more than men.

LIVING ON HIGH ALERT

So, for those of you in the business of customer care, you need to understand how women think about what they buy and what influences their loyalty. Women have great social power to influence other spenders around them. Women also appreciate a brand story that triggers an emotional connection for them. They buy what they feel good about.

Unilever's Dove created many popular and powerful marketing campaigns that connect with female audiences at a core emotional level – far better than a direct-selling approach. Their commercials are aimed at celebrating beauty and self-esteem for every body (not necessarily women only) despite their differences in shape, ethnicity, gender or age. In 2013, Dove's *Real Beauty Sketches* campaign explored how women perceive themselves versus how others see them through the use of portraits drawn by an FBI forensic artist. The results were surprising to their subjects and the words "You are more beautiful than you think" rang loud and clear in the end. The ad went viral and was viewed nearly 163 million times globally. Depicting women the way they want to see themselves will lead them to see the company in the same way.

Recently, **Brawny paper towels** *launched a series of short films starring accomplished women sharing their empowering personal stories of breaking through the gender stereotype - a woman doing a man's work - who then strike the Brawny Man pose in the red-plaid shirt. This woman-centric ad campaign from one of the manliest brand icons in advertisement history – next to the Marlboro Man, Dos Equis Most Interesting Man in the World, Mr. Clean and Old Spice – wants women to know that you don't have to be a man to have Brawny strength.*

DOES THIS APPLY TO B2B?

Some of you might be saying, "That might work for clothing and groceries but I'm in the B2B space." Ok, then you should know that female influence is not limited to consumer goods. Women influence a growing percentage of business-to-business transactions as well.

In an article from A.T. Kerney, a UK trends and marketing consultancy was quoted as saying, "Women control a growing share of B2B spending. UK companies can gain a competitive advantage by successfully connecting with female buyers. We see emerging evidence of the same differences in buying behaviour in the B2B space (as in B2C). A recently released study of more than 600 board directors in Canada found that women were more inquisitive than men and more likely to consider the interests of multiple stakeholders. At the same time, it reported that women attach less importance than men to rituals (such as being wined and dined by top executives) and feel less constrained by rules, regulations, and traditional ways of doing business. US research found that women in purchasing are more attuned than men to particular aspects of the sales and customer management process, especially the frequency of buyer-seller communications."

MOST UNHAPPY CUSTOMERS DON'T COMPLAIN. THEY JUST LEAVE.

As you might guess, the majority of customers don't complain - they just stop buying from you. Customers who submit an intentional complaint are the icy tip of a nasty iceberg of lost business. Complainers not only want their voice to be heard but on some level they think of themselves as the spokespeople for the silent majority. Many are eager to take the time to write a letter, post a blog, or leave a voicemail about why the world doesn't like you.

RELAX: ANGRY, COMPLAINT-HAPPY CUSTOMERS ARE _NOT_ LOST TO YOU FOREVER

This may be astonishing to some of you. We've all read Avaya stats that claim, "Due to the global choices we have today 73 percent of buyers between 24-54 years of age will bolt to a competitor after a single mistake." While I believe that to be true, the more relevant question is, "Can we salvage an angry customer?"

The answer is YES...if the customer has had a decent "relationship" with you in the past. Let me explain. If the customer has never seen you before and you blow it, they will probably dash off to a competitor. But if you have established some rapport and trust with the customer, you have a shot at recovering the customer.

In a separate survey from "The Customer Shouts Back," I wanted to know what percentage of customers would stop buying from a company as a result of extremely poor treatment. Only 12 percent said they would never go back (if they had a relationship with you). Really? That means 88 percent of badly treated customers could be resurrected.

Even at your worst, there's a sliver of hope in the customer's mind about doing business with you again. They want this thing to work out because it's too much trouble researching other brands and vendors. Of the 12 percent who said they would never come back, only three percent threatened to file a lawsuit if they didn't get resolution. I urge you to believe that while three percent is small, it is not an acceptable loss. Fix the customer's problem (to their notion of satisfaction) and they will come back.

CHAPTER 5

BEWARE! SOME CUSTOMERS CAN BE EXTREMELY IRRATIONAL

YOUR CUSTOMERS MIGHT ACTUALLY BE A BIT CRAZY

Since the last chapter dealt with epic complainers I thought it would be important for you to know that not all complaints are *your* fault. Sometimes, erratic behavior belongs to the customer.

You try really hard to make sure the customer has a wonderful experience with you and then…something sets them off. You think, *"What the…?"* I'm sure you've had customer interactions that left you thinking, *"That made no sense at all. He's (she's) crazy!"* Well, you're right. People can be a tad "mental" whenever they spend their hard-earned money.

Daniel Kahneman won a Nobel Prize in behavioral economics by studying how human nature and emotions cause people to make irrational decisions. Basically,

Kahneman's "prospect theory" shines a light on the idea that your customers are not very good at calculating the odds of losing money, gaining money, or spending money wisely. People would rather avoid a loss than take a shot at an extremely easy gain. This explains why customers get so crazed when they think they have lost money on a purchase from you.

Colin Camerer, an economist at the California Institute of Technology, wrote an article called "Prospect Theory in the Wild" where he described how Kahneman's prospect theory applied to New York City cab drivers' earning behavior.

> "Many New York City cab drivers decide when to finish work each day by setting themselves a daily income target, (let's say \$125/day). Upon reaching the \$125 goal they stopped working. This means that they typically work shorter hours on a busy day than they do on a slow day. Rational labor market theory predicts that they will do the opposite (work longer hours on a busy day to make a lot more money but they don't). Quitting early seems like irrational behavior."

The same can be said about internal customers (your coworkers). Many salespeople will work hard to meet their sales quota. But, if they meet that quota early in the month, they start slacking off rather than working even harder to make more money.

Kahneman and Camerer offer these examples to explain why customers become irrational when they think they have been cheated on a purchase. If you took a customer's money and didn't give them what *they* expected, you risk hitting their emotional trip wire.

When they buy, customers have highly emotional motives in mind.

To gain a higher social status
To appear thinner
To stay out of trouble
To have more hair
To look smart to the boss
To attract attention
To become an expert
To reduce stress
To experience an exotic resort
To impress a girlfriend or boyfriend
To overcome depression

Secondly, social scientists tell us that customer spending habits can look totally illogical.

The customer owns a Mercedes Benz automobile yet shops at Walmart.

A customer will walk a block to save $100 on a $1,000 computer but won't walk the same block to save $1000 on a $25,000 car.

TIME PRESSURE

Every purchase has the potential to be an emotional transaction for us when the decision must be made within a short time frame. Time pressure can cause an emotional reaction that escalates itself. That's why you see so many TV ads that shout, "Prices will only be this low during our 12-hour sale" or "We are absolutely closing our doors forever at midnight." Customers don't act rationally when the pressure to buy "on sale" is exacerbated by a time constraint.

BECOME A CUSTOMER PSYCHOLOGIST

Beyond collecting terabytes of Big Data on our customers, we need to know the customer's emotional state when they are trying to buy from us. In the course of any transaction there could be great WOWs and devastating POWs. Either reaction creates a customer mood swing. You can prevent much of this customer angst by learning how to read a person's mood throughout the transaction.

CAN YOU "READ" PEOPLE?

Face reading is an art that is practiced by people like renowned jury consultant Jo-Ellen Dimitrius, PhD. The American Bar Association calls Dimitrius "the pre-trial pro" because she is highly skilled at studying faces and body language for the purpose of assembling "friendly" jurors for her clients. If you want to know her tricks-of-the-trade, read her book, "Reading People."

Wouldn't you like to know if your customer came to you scared, angry, reluctant, or irritated--even without saying a single word to you? Maybe you have noticed another person's moods (all of your life) but just haven't officially identified the emotions. Some call it intuition.

At one of your staff meetings, try playing an emotional guessing game. Write down a list of emotions on 3X5 cards (one emotion per card) and ask each person to demonstrate the facial expression on the card. Everyone else has to guess your mood. Here are some emotions to write on each card.

SAD	FRUSTRATED	SNEAKY
HAPPY	JEALOUS	SHADY
DISGUSTED	DISORIENTED	CONFIDENT
AFRAID	CONFUSED	DEVIOUS
IRRITATED	SMOLDERING	SHY
SARCASTIC	HURT	CONTEMPT

Before long you'll notice that you are trying to figure out the facial expressions of your friends, your relatives, and total strangers in your local grocery store. You'll discover that you aren't talking as much as you used to. Instead, you are listening and observing more.

CAUTION: This game may not work with people who've just gotten Botox. (If you laughed, you were supposed to.)

WHAT HAPPENS WHEN IRRATIONAL CUSTOMERS COMPLAIN ONLINE?

Since emotions can easily flare, the customer interaction could escalate. An out-of-control POW moment is dangerous because these days, customers love to catch people misbehaving – and then document it. Everyone has a cell phone camera and customers feel they are doing a public service by taking a movie of YOU messing up. Not kidding, here! You should always be aware that a single person with a large social media network could launch a complaint that goes viral. This is the best reason not to bring your bad mood to work. If you mistreat a customer, your "episode" could go public to thousands or hundreds of thousands of people. It is always wise to assume that your behavior is being caught on camera.

ELECTRONIC MOOD READING

For those of you working for larger companies it is impossible to study literally millions of customer responses by hand. Luckily, technology has developed electronic listening software. Social listening software companies like Kana Software can "hear" the mood of a customer complaint. Listening software can detect anger, happiness, frustration and about two dozen other emotions. If a written complaint is submitted through a website, text, or letter, the software breaks down the customer's words (and phrases) to decipher the customer's frame of mind. It is important to know the customer's emotional state at the time of the infraction so that your company can respond correctly without escalating the situation. Here's what I find astonishing. The software can literally analyze hundreds of thousands of complaints a minute.

Someday, I hope someone invents a mood scanning wand we can just pass over our customer's head. That way if they get too agitated we can use the wand to bat them upside the head (just kidding).

HOW TO ESCAPE THE INSANITY

If the customer's temper suddenly explodes and you just cannot understand their logic, don't argue with them. All you can do is let them vent. After the customer has calmed down, you can neutralize the situation by saying, "I understand why you are angry and I would be too in your situation. What can I do to make this right?"

It's pretty hard to argue with someone who wants to make things right.

CHAPTER 6

LEARNING TO LOVE COMPLAINTS

When I get a consulting assignment, the first thing I ask to see (and hear) are the complaints. Customer complaints are a window into the soul of your organizational culture. Complaints aren't surveys. Complaints are the specific feedback that identifies where time was stolen and what you *didn't* do about it.

Sit in a room for a week with all of your complaint letters, texts, and phone calls. Next, catalog every single misstep and look for a pattern.

Now, make a list of every complaint – at every customer interaction point (some people call them customer touch points) – and then propose a correcting action.

It might look like this:

COMPLAINT: Nobody was available to help me when I walked into the office.

CORRECTION: If the receptionist is out to lunch or running errands, we need a motion sensor light (or bell) to alert us that someone has entered the office. Nobody should be ignored or neglected when they visit us.

COMPLAINT: Nobody answered the phone after six rings. When the person did pick up, he was rude and short with me.

CORRECTION: We need to train people to pick up the phone within three rings.

COMPLAINT: This is the second time my order was shipped with the wrong parts.

CORRECTION: We need a double-check quality control procedure for every order that leaves the warehouse. For accountability reasons we should include a "last-checked by sheet" and the person's name who checked the order before shipping.

Be as detailed about the process as you can. Write down every customer handoff, every customer expectation, and every customer failure. Where and when did your process fall through the cracks? What can you do (or say) to insure this mistake never happens again? I assure you, your scores will rise if you remove the friction from every customer interaction. You may want to design a customer journey map.

CUSTOMER JOURNEY MAPPING

You may already be savvy to the benefits of "customer journey mapping." If not, here's an introduction that should whet your appetite. The customer map is fun and colorful and could be mistaken for the old *Chutes and Ladders* game. In fact, it just occurred to me that Chutes and Ladders would make a sensational customer journey game. Your customer works really hard to make it to the top, and one wrong move (by you) and the customer falls from potential success to instant failure.

The idea is to write out each step in the customer's journey and convert it to a sort of trail map. Every time a customer goes from one point of company interaction to another (let's say from online product purchase - to software activation – to call center support) there is a predetermined behavior enacted (by you) which is designed to cause a positive emotional outcome for the customer.

Here's where most journey maps fall short. The customer journey steps are defined but the customer's emotional reaction to each step is not. It is critical that we identify anything that causes customer friction. When we know if the customer is feeling WOWed or POWed, the customer engagement team can make course corrections to smooth out the process. See the appendix to learn how to install customer journey mapping for your company.

BE DETACHED & BRUTAL

What I am suggesting above can be laborious. It takes time and an open mind. If you and your team members are honest with each other about what you can do better, you will see the results sooner than you expected.

Conversely, I've seen companies try this exercise and fail because they didn't want to hurt anybody's feelings by bringing up mistakes. This is not the time to sugarcoat or minimize missteps. Somebody has to stand up and say, "We are here to eliminate all of the friction between us, our processes, and our customers. There is no blame here. Just improvement."

That should put everyone at ease and redirect the focus on the prize, which is to underscore that Time Lost and Customer Friction must be eliminated so that your company can make more money and accumulate more lifetime customers.

It is the responsibility of each customer-facing person to audit his or her own behavior.

(This also applies to internal customers (coworkers.)

THE ONGOING REMINDER

I hope you always remember to ask yourself, "Am I committing WOW behavior or POW behavior?" If it's POW behavior, self-correct before the transaction is over.

If you are a team leader or project manager, you have to get your team to face reality and systematically identify the specific moments of customer friction.

This is a crucial reminder because your actions can truly save your company from disaster.

In the first chapter I teased you with a thumbnail sketch of the Comcast resurrection story. Here are more details related to how they returned a dying company to growth.

COMCAST FIXED EVERYTHING

Comcast is the largest cable and broadband provider in the U.S. Unfortunately, the company was among the lowest-ranking in customer service and satisfaction scores. In mid-2014, Comcast made front-page news when an AOL executive called Comcast customer service to cancel his service. After recording and posting his horribly frustrating 18-minute-long argument with a call center retention specialist, more than five million people took a stand and voiced their opinion on Comcast's lack of customer care. The company said the call led to mandatory employee-coaching courses and training materials "to reinforce that the overall customer experience is our top priority." Comcast listened to the complaints from all angles.

> By the end of 2015, Comcast launched a $300 million upgrade. They added service technicians and technology to integrate their cable, Internet, and phone billing services. In the first year, this wholesale transformation to a customer-centric mindset expanded their workforce and call centers - and sped up response times by 18 percent. For the first time in eight years, they added 1.4 million new Internet customers and profits grew more than two percent to $1.97 billion - their best year in nearly 10 years. The company said their recent investments and open relationship with their customers over social media have helped their reputation grow exponentially. Comcast customers now say they have more convenience and choice.

I love that story because it underscores the hope that we can recover customers we've disappointed. The reason we can get them back has to do with human nature. Oddly, our customers do not separate their business reactions from their personal feelings. Why do your personal relationships get rocky? Why do they end? Maybe your "friend" lied to you, betrayed you, humiliated you or was constantly negative. Maybe your "friend" didn't do anything except neglect you? And, then how many times have you kissed and made up? (Why do you think so many jewelry stores and flower shops flourish?)

Never assume a customer thinks of you as "just business." Secretly they want to rekindle a relationship with you so they can stop "dating" your competition.

BTW: CUSTOMERS AREN'T SCORING THE COMPANY

You may think a poor customer score is aimed at the company. But actually, when customers complain, they are complaining and scoring *you, the customer-facing person*. In the research I did for my book "Customer Empathy," I learned that a customer's emotional state (at the time they interacted with you) determines how they score *your* performance. Think of what a customer has gone through before they ever intersected with you (in person, on the phone, or through email). That customer has lived a whole life before it was your turn to be a part of it.

CHAPTER 7

EXECUTING THE PERFECT CUSTOMER EXPERIENCE

The perfect customer experience is one that makes the customer feel important and valuable. (Who doesn't like that?) The customer is overjoyed when you show extreme interest in them, *not* YOURSELF. I'm talking about the humanity of the customer experience – something data can't tell you.

FIRST IMPRESSIONS SET THE TONE

How do newcomers perceive your company?

When a customer first visits your company online, in person, or over the phone, it is crucial that their first impression is not stained by a bitter, short-fused, belligerent grump. Your in-person brand persona must be consistent with the brand you project publicly. Branding starts with hiring the right personalities in reception, admin, and security. Easier said than done?

FROM SELF-CENTERED TO OTHER-CENTERED

Sadly, too many of us get so wrapped up in our own lives that we don't spend much time practicing how to care about other people. I blame social media because Facebook, Twitter, Instagram, and others have convinced us that the world can't wait to hear what we've been doing every two hours. We post our relationship troubles, our hobbies, our medical conditions, our party photos, cute animal videos we found and we even take pictures of our food so other people can see what we are eating. I know. Ridiculous. No wonder we don't put other people first... we are swamped with talking about ourselves! A customer-centric culture requires you to put *your* needs and wants on hold while you serve others.

When I find a person who exemplifies other-centeredness I post that story on social media to remind us the world is full of customers who need our attention more than we do.

Incidentally, the person in this story is so memorable, I guarantee that after one read through you'll instantly be able to tell this story to your coworkers.

FROM CUBA WITH LOVE

A few years ago, I met a young woman who should be the national spokeswoman for customer-centricity. I had been travelling for a week across the United States giving speeches. At the end of that week I checked into the Orlando World Center Marriott at midnight, famished. Against my better judgment of eating late I opened the room service menu and saw the most beautiful photograph of a bacon cheeseburger. I couldn't resist. But I ordered a Diet Coke just so I wouldn't be adding unnecessary calories (yeah, it's a mind game I play with myself). I was told my order would be there in 30 minutes but 22 minutes later there was a knock at my door. A pleasant young woman entered with a tray and, seriously, the photograph of the burger didn't do this masterpiece justice.

The burger was huge and surrounded by hot golden steak fries the size of bananas. Next to that was a tall, ice-cold glass of Diet...Pepsi? I must have looked a little disappointed because the young woman said, "I'm so sorry we are out of Diet Coke in the kitchen. We've had a big convention. I hope Diet Pepsi is okay?" I was polite but told her I was only fussy about one thing: I prefer the taste of Coke to Pepsi...but I was grateful she also brought water. She apologized all the way out the door.

I bit into a steak fry – best ever. Burger? The bacon was crispy. The meat and melted jack cheese were hot, juicy, and nestled between a soft oversized sesame seed bun. Heaven. Not even 30 seconds later, there was another knock on my door and the same room service woman was holding an ice cold Diet Coke. I said, "I thought you were out of those?" She said, "We are out in the kitchen but I found this in a machine four floors down." I was stunned. I tried to pay for it but she wouldn't take my money. She said, "I just want to make sure you're happy here." She leaves but I can't let this go.

I pick up the phone and call room service, "Who was the woman who just delivered my bacon cheeseburger?" A male voice says, "That was Maria Garcia. I hope there isn't a problem. She is just here from Cuba and...." I interrupted, "No problem at all. In fact, I coach companies about customer engagement and I have to tell you what she did (I rave for several minutes). The voice on the line said, "Would you mind saying something to the hotel manager?"

I said, "Well I was going to have a bacon cheeseburger but since I'm working for you now, I'm on it." I not only talked to the hotel manager, I praised Maria Garcia in a letter I wrote to Marriott International. I even recreated that scene for one of my retail human resource customer training films. To me, this was a customer service story of epic proportions.

What most impressed me about Maria was this: In a glimpse, she noticed the disappointment on my face when she delivered a replacement soda. I dismissed it when I saw the burger. But she didn't. She only thought about how she could correct a misstep. Her mission was to find a Diet Coke, no matter what. And for that dollar she must have spent on a diet Coke, Marriott not only got a lifetime customer...but a viral story. My YouTube video telling this story has nearly 300,000 views.

What happened to Maria Garcia? Well, when I went back to that hotel a year later to give Maria the HR video about her and share some letters from clients who loved her story, I found out that she is now the food and beverage manager at one of Marriott's northeastern properties. Not a surprise, really. Customers are so impressed with other-centered behavior that they talk about you...like I did. And, your employer is so impressed that they want your behavior to rub off on other team members...even if it means promoting you to leadership.

The best part of the Maria Garcia story is how finely tuned in she was to my mood. My disappointment only surfaced for a glimpse but she saw it and was bent on doing something about it. She could "read" people. Considering her humble background I doubt that Maria Garcia had the formal training of a jury consultant but I'd bet she's spent a lifetime paying attention to other people.

The side effect of studying other people (and their apparent moods) is that you are not focusing your mind's energy on YOURSELF. Do it long enough and you'll become an other-centered person. (A little known fact is that other-centered people have the most and best friends.)

CHAPTER 8

EMPOWERING FRICTION-FREE SOLUTIONS

EMPOWER ON-DEMAND AUTHORITY

To remove customer friction, senior leaders need to give every team member the responsibility for diffusing a customer's anxiety, on-demand.

Leadership must also give every team member the authority to carry out that mission.

There isn't a one-size-fits-all customer solution. Regardless of the variables, senior leaders and YOU need to agree upon several appropriate solutions to keep your customer happy. Will it take a full refund, a two-for-one coupon, a bigger discount, a credit, a replacement item, a gift, free assembly or shipping, or an extra service? You must also have the authority to let the customer dictate what will make them happy—within a reasonable limit that you and your leaders agree upon.

If the outcome is a satisfied customer, then *you* (the customer-facing person) are the one who must have the authority to make that happen. Below is what I'd call a really smart Win-Win solution.

THERE IS NO GUARANTEE YOUR TEAM WILL WIN

A good friend of mine is the chief customer experience officer for an NBA basketball team. He has over 18,000 "customers" in his arena every time his team takes the court. His challenge is to make sure his customers have a great experience in light of the fact that he can't guarantee that your favorite team will win the game. Add to that, he has 300 non-paid volunteers working to ensure that ticket holders have a great experience. As you may know, an NBA game is non-stop entertainment. Music is booming. Cheerleaders are dancing. Balloon drones and T-shirt cannons fire prizes into the air. A half-court shoot off contest exhilarates the crowd. As fun as this environment is designed to be, things can go wrong. Fans drink too much. They throw hot dogs. And sometimes, they get into fistfights with each other. One way to ruin an evening at the arena is to have a rowdy fan spill beer or smear mustard on your nice shirt. My friend had the perfect solution. All 300 of his volunteers keep a lookout for freshly stained clothing. If they spot a clothing accident each volunteer is empowered to give away a team logo T-shirt to the afflicted fan...for free. My friend says they only give out three to four T-shirts a game...and the best thing is to have turned a POW moment into a WOW experience. Who wouldn't like to leave the arena wearing their team's name on a brand new shirt? Which company wouldn't want their fans to become walking billboards for their brand?

EMPOWERMENT IS NOT EXPENSIVE

Remember the energy company client I talked about earlier?

The most surprising customer experience glitch I found was that team members (linemen, call center representatives, tree trimmers, designers) didn't believe they were empowered to make those on-the-spot decisions to correct a customer POW moment. They (unwittingly) thought if they tried to help a customer and were wrong, they would get chewed out by the boss.

I asked senior leaders why they didn't give the authority to these folks. The leaders said, "We just assumed they knew they were supposed to make the customer happy."

I learned long ago that we cannot assume behavior to be automatic.

SIDE STORY: When I was producing customer service training films, I had a client tell me, "We love the film but you didn't tell our wait staff to smile. Can you shoot a scene like that?" I learned that leaders have to spell out the behavior they want replicated.

Back to the energy company.

To clarify encouraging the troops to make things right with the customer, every time we held a meeting, one of the senior leaders would say, "We want you to know that we support you taking care of the customer. Do whatever you have to do to make the customer happy." This was a great first step... but it wasn't quite a complete solution.

If you're a power pole lineman, how do you interpret the phrase, "...whatever you have to do?" There needed to be absolute clarity, specifically in terms of the financial value parameters of "whatever you have to do."

Surprisingly, when I asked the power linemen and tree trimmers what they thought was a fair customer peace offering, they all guessed a much lower dollar figure than management was willing to offer. The company was willing to pay up to $250 per customer to make them happy. The field teams thought a $25-$50 energy credit toward a customer's electric bill would be plenty. Cutting loose a few bucks is cheap money. In the grand scheme of staying in business, this is not an expense.

It's re-marketing to keep customers.

I've got another case study that demonstrates (1) the importance of understanding the customer's perspective and (2) why leadership has to articulate the consequences of empowerment with extreme clarity.

I was hired by a large casino chain that wanted to raise their customer experience scores. As usual, I started by examining the customer complaints. Most customer complaints arose when employees would say things like:

"I'm sorry but that's not my job"

"There is nothing else I can do"

"There is nobody here to help you. Can you call back tomorrow?" "It's not our policy to do that."

"That isn't my fault."

Next, I asked a group of team members to come up with what they thought the customer felt when they heard these statements.

WHAT WAS SAID: "I'm sorry but that's not my job."
WHAT THE CUSTOMER PROBABLY FELT: They must have thought we didn't know anyone who could fix the problem. We should know everyone in our department so that we direct the customer to the right place.

WHAT WAS SAID: "There is nothing else I can do."
WHAT THE CUSTOMER PROBABLY FELT: That was probably the worst thing a customer could hear because it rendered the situation hopeless. We should always have some option to help them. We should rehearse better answers so we can solve the problem sooner.

WHAT WAS SAID: "Can you call back tomorrow?"
WHAT THE CUSTOMER PROBABLY FELT: We probably just extended the customer's pain. We need to know how to solve problems immediately.

WHAT I SAID: "It's not our policy to do that."
WHAT THE CUSTOMER PROBABLY FELT: The customer must have felt like we poked a sharp stick in his/her eye. They probably thought, "what kind of policy is worth losing a customer like me?"

WHAT I SAID: "That isn't our fault."
WHAT THE CUSTOMER PROBABLY FELT: The customer must have thought we were blaming them for the problem. They should have used Ross's phrase, "I know you're angry and I would be too if I were you. But what can I do to resolve this right now?"

Next, I asked management, "What can your team members do to turn a POW moment into a WOW experience?" Management gave me a specific dollar amount they said was acceptable for saving a customer. But before I told the team what management considered a reasonable make-people-happy budget, I asked the team members, "What would it take to make an angry customer happy? Twenty dollars? Fifty dollars?" The most common answer was, "If I could offer the customer a free drink or a $25 gift certificate toward a dinner, they would be blown away." When I revealed, "Management says you can offer them up to $200," they were blown away! When they discovered they could offer the value of a free dinner, a free massage, free movie tickets, and even a free overnight stay, there was great relief in the room. One person said, "I can make anyone happy with a $200 budget."

For those of you who think customers will take advantage of your generosity, or if employees will give their friends free meals, settle your mind. One leader told me, "I'm totally comfortable with giving our team members leeway. They know our customers well enough that they will know if our customers are trying to squeeze us out of money."

EL CAJON HARLEY EMPOWERS PEOPLE

My friend Randy bought a new motorcycle from El Cajon Harley-Davidson near San Diego, CA. Before Randy took the bike home he decided to have some extra chrome accessories installed. (A common affliction for Harley buyers). The installation was going to take a few days so he'd come back on the weekend. Two days later, my friend woke up in a cold sweat, terrified. Randy couldn't remember seeing the letters EFI on the air cleaner (EFI stands for electronic fuel injection). So now Randy was thinking he bought a carbureted model; which wasn't what he intended. He jumped to the conclusion that the shop had already installed accessories on the wrong motorcycle. In a panic, he called the El Cajon parts technician and said, "I think we may have a problem." The technician's voice interrupted Randy to say, "Let me reassure you, whatever it is, there is no problem. We will make sure you are the happiest biker who ever left our shop."

The technician had immediately removed the friction and Randy's heartbeat returned to normal when the technician assured him he'd bought the EFI model. Crisis averted due to expert empowerment.

CHAPTER 9

THE LOYALTY MOMENT OF ANY TRANSACTION

THE FINAL MOMENT

You go to a live stage show and the ending is so amazing that you give the actors a standing ovation.

You watch a fireworks display and when the explosions speed up you hear the audience yelling, "Here comes the finale!"

You watch the final season episode of your favorite TV series and your emotions are held captive by the cliff-hanger. You can't wait until the next season starts.

I liken the customer's memory of their final moment to what psychologists refer to as the "recency effect." The recency effect is a recall phenomenon. When people are asked to remember the items on a list (in any order), those that come at the end of the list are more likely to be recalled than the others. This speaks to the notion that we remember the last things we saw, heard, or felt better than what we experienced first.

The recency effect is consistent with how we rate our other memories.

In a love relationship, when you leave the house in the morning the way your partner kisses you goodbye imprints you with a feeling. Maybe it's a warm feeling... Or maybe your "sixth sense" tells you something is wrong... Maybe you sense underlying frustration? Well, that feeling isn't dismissed. You think about it - maybe all day - until you resolve the feeling through conversation.

All of these are examples demonstrating the power of The Final Moment. But, we haven't been taught to apply the recency effect to our businesses...until now. I promise if you apply the power of the final moment, your customer scores will rise.

Here's how to do it.

As you are saying goodbye to a customer, or closing out a transaction, we need to perform something memorable. We need to smile. We need to thank people for their business. We need to say, "Before we close this out, is there anything else I can do for you?"

What happens next is that your customers form an associative memory about experiencing YOU. Since YOU are the last person in the transaction, they will subconsciously catalog how much or how little friction they encountered by dealing with you. Customers remember satisfying experiences and will subconsciously keep going back to the same person, product, or service hoping to repeat that great experience.

Be creative in the final customer moment. Surprise them. Delight them. Make them remember you.

Now, don't forget to find a nice place to erect your reminder signs.

RESPECT TIME.

CUSTOMER FRICTION.

WOW.

POW.

CHAPTER 10

YOUR BLUEPRINT IS READY

I promised to give you a bold blueprint to boost your customer scores. For easy reference, shoot this page with your camera phone.

1. Start with a baseline customer satisfaction score. The system you are currently using is fine. Remind everyone that your immediate goals are to RESPECT YOUR CUSTOMER'S TIME and ELIMINATE ALL CUSTOMER FRICTION.

2. Start using the words WOW and POW as simple identifiers to describe your behaviors. "Did I execute a WOW moment or did I commit a POW moment?"

3. Course correct as necessary.

4. Faithfully log every one of your formal complaints (written and voice) so that you can sniff out the recurring problems in your system.

5. Become keenly aware of your customer's moods and emotional states so that you'll know how to deal with angry or frustrated customers. If you use electronic listening software, dig into the "mood" data so that you can gauge the intensity of their angst.

6. Plot corrective actions to repair each and every CUSTOMER FRICTION point. I suggest designing a Customer Journey Map accompanied by the customer's emotional trigger points along the path. Attaching emotions underscores the levels of importance of each trigger point mishap.

7. Once you have devised deliberate actions that effectively smooth out the repeat offenses, you need senior leadership to deliver the news to everyone with extreme clarity. There is no room for misinterpretation.

8. Discuss behavior modification with the appropriate team members. Getting the behaviors right may require a dedicated re-training effort.

9. Empower team members to make on-demand decisions in favor of the customer. No problems. No waiting. No unhappy customers.

Follow this blueprint for higher customer satisfaction, customer engagement, and customer experience scores.

APPENDIX

CHAPTER 1:
COMPARING CUSTOMER SATISFACTION
MEASUREMENT SYSTEMS

J.D. Power is the leader for comparing competitive companies within an industry. They compare and rate companies against each other based on:

- Overall customer satisfaction through consumer surveys of product and/or service quality

- Buyer behavior

- Consumers' familiarity with products and programs (advertising, incentives)

- Ease of management (consumers' access to technology and support)

- Going beyond (awareness, education)

J.D. Power studies serve as a benchmark for quality/customer satisfaction measurements. They compare your company scores with others in your industry. J.D. Power information is collected from real customers. The information is independent and verified. The feedback is unbiased; not answering to a customer forum or chat room. Third party feedback is more credible and clear. Consumers feel that they can make more informed decisions when they see how a company stacks up against the competition.

Magnet Status Hospital: This designation assesses a hospital's prolonged kindness and humanity. There is an expensive two-year process for a hospital to receive "Magnet Designation." The reason it is called "Magnet" is that allegedly your hospital is so good that you become a magnet for nurses.

The Magnet Recognition Program is based on 14 characteristics or "Forces of Magnetism" in five groups:

1. Transformational leadership (advocacy and support by influential leadership)
   - Respecting the patient; being courteous; putting the patient in charge of decision-making

2. Structural empowerment (shared decision-making to establish standards for improvement – partnerships

with their patients and medical teams)
- Listening to and educating the patient

3. Exemplary professional practice (complete plan of care, quality monitoring, ensured effectiveness using the improvement model)
- Explaining the plan of action for maintaining Magnet status

4. New knowledge innovation & improvements (practice to generate new knowledge)

5. Empirical quality results (outcomes demonstrating excellence)
- Surveys, asking questions, response and follow-up

Net Promoter Scores (NPS) by Frederich Reicheld, author of "The Ultimate Question," has had enormous recent adoption by Fortune 500 companies. It is based upon a two-question evaluation system. Q#1: Using a 0-10 rating, how likely would you recommend us to your friends? Q#2: What did we do that caused you to rate us like you did in Q#1?

Respondents are grouped as follows: (1) Promoters (score 9-10) are loyal customers who will keep buying and recommend you to others. (2) Passives (score 7-8) are satisfied but open to your competition. (3) Detractors (score

0-6) are dissatisfied customers who can bruise your brand and corrupt your company through negative word-of-mouth. If you subtract the percentage of Detractors from the percentage of Promoters, you have your NPS.

Pros: It's easy to convince someone to answer one question.

Cons: There is no proof your promoters actually will recommend you in real life; the question is generic – it's not easy to pinpoint improvement areas without an open-ended follow-up question.

Customers are more likely to share negative experiences than positive ones. Focus on the negative feedback – by monitoring your Detractors and getting them back to Passive or Promoter-level scores, you can enhance your NPS score. Ask, listen, and respond!

In order to improve NPS, measure the customer's opinions across different channels. Create multiple contact moments and experiences through social media and email. Use open-ended questions to follow-up on the single question. Provide high quality service to generate loyalty and get referrals. And don't forget to reward customers for promoting and spreading the good word about your company.

CSAT (Customer SATisfaction) covers a range of questions tailored to each company or situation in relation to a specific transaction. If you're measuring a single transaction the question is: *"How would you rate your overall satisfaction with the service you received?"* There is a 1 to 5 grading scale, with 1 representing "very dissatisfied" and 5 representing "very satisfied." The average customer response is the CSAT score. Some organizations set a standard and a less than desirable score prompts further action.

Pros: Beyond a single transaction, CSAT allows you to ask customers a variety of questions to better understand more complex problems.

Cons: A single transaction does not always reflect a company-wide effort like "improve customer experience." If customers are not really engaged, they may answer in the middle of the grading scale or not answer all of the questions.

CSAT focuses on short-term happiness from a specific interaction. A respectful interaction leads to a positive customer reaction and increased customer satisfaction. CSAT recommends the following method for treating customers better.

- Treat your customers like they're your boss; thank them, go out of your way to impress them, and above all, keep your promises.

- Update your website; include info on what you sell or services rendered, options provided and why customers want to buy what you offer in a user-friendly, easily accessible website.

- Focus on customer interaction. Open yourself to community engagement through marketing campaigns and social media. The customer should be listened to and understood – people with a respectful experience are more likely to be repeat customers and share their experience with others.

- Talk to the customer to determine what they want and deliver. Under-promise, don't over-deliver (it's better to meet, not necessarily exceed, their expectations than to fail or disappoint them). Keep it simple, make it positive, ask for more feedback/criticism, and act on insight.

- Be loyal: remember special occasions, empower customers by investing in self-service support channels and educate.

A Customer Effort Score (CES) grades how much effort a customer put into an interaction with your company. "How much effort did you personally have to put forth to handle your request?" They may also ask if the company made it easy for the customer to handle his/her issue. Answers range from very low effort (1) to high effort (5). Research from the creators of the Customer Effort Score showed that, "Service organizations create loyal customers primarily by reducing customer effort – i.e. helping them solve their problems quickly and easily – not by delighting them in service interactions."

Pros: Makes it easier to find improvement areas. According to CES research, 94 percent of customers who have a low-effort service experience will buy from that same company again.

Cons: CES does not account for what actually made a transaction easy/difficult, whether it was the price or a problem with the product itself.

A high average means your company is making things easy for your customers. Too low means customers are putting in too much effort to interact with you. To improve CES, look for patterns of issues and head off the problem in advance. For example, are you switching your customers to different departments too often? If so, make appropriate workflow changes. Implement self-service: assume a customer can answer some of their own questions if you provide them with the proper tools (a website and/or IVR automated system). Make sure the technology is working, is easy to navigate, and ensure access to a live person who can capture notes, provide step-by-step resolutions and explain the issue (don't make them repeat their complaint again).

REFERENCES

CHAPTER 1:
THE COMCAST COMEBACK http://www.timesfreepress.com/news/business/aroundregion/story/2015/oct/25/comcast-spends-300-million-adds-workers-improve-customer-service/332468/

http://nypost.com/2016/02/03/comcast-says-fixing-its-horrible-customer-service-is-paying-off/

http://motherboard.vice.com/read/comcast-investigating-customer-service-call-from-hell

THE GREAT LEGO TURNAROUND
http://www.businessinsider.com/how-lego-made-a-huge-turn-around-2014-2

J.D. POWER COMPARES COMPETITORS
http://www.jdpower.com/about-us/faq-general-questions

MAGNET HOSPITALS

https://en.wikipedia.org/wiki/Magnet_Recognition_Program

http://www.mghpcs.org/eed_portal/Documents/PatExp/magnet-imprvpln-tipsheet.pdf

http://www.nursecredentialing.org/Magnet/ProgramOverview/New-Magnet-Model.aspx

CUSTOMER EXPERIENCE SCORING COMPARISONS - NPS, CSAT, CES

http://www.customerexperienceupdate.com/customer-experience/nps/?open-article-id=4818619&article-title=nps--csat--or-ces--whats-the-true-measure-of-customer-loyalty-&blog-domain=cx-journey.com&blog-title=cx-journey

https://www.checkmarket.com/blog/csat-ces-nps-compared/

http://www.customerexperienceupdate.com/nps/report/?open-article-id=4818619&article-title=nps--csat--or-ces--what-s-the-true-measure-of-customer-loyalty-&blog-domain=cx-journey.com&blog-title=cx-journey

http://www.netpromotersystem.com/about/measuring-your-net-promoter-score.aspx

http://www.teamhgs.com/blog/4-steps-to-improving-customer-effort-scores-ces/

http://www.evergage.com/blog/3-ways-improve-net-promoter-scores/

https://hbr.org/2010/07/stop-trying-to-delight-your-customers

AMAZON GO GROCERY

https://www.youtube.com/watch?v=NrmMk1Myrxc

UBER REDUCES ALL FRICTION
https://techcrunch.com/2011/10/16/reduce-friction-increase-happiness/

ON DEMAND DOCTORS: "THE DOCTOR WILL SKYPE YOU NOW"
http://health.usnews.com/health-news/patient-advice/articles/2014/08/06/the-doctor-will-skype-you-now

THE CUSTOMER SHOUTS BACK by Ross Shafer
https://www.amazon.com/Customer-Shouts-Back-Ross-Shafer/dp/1598580620/ref=sr_1_fkmr0_1?s=books&ie=UTF8&qid=1490155665&sr=1-1-fkmr0&keywords=customer+shoots+back+ross+shafer

CHAPTER 2:
SAMSUNG PHONES ON FIRE
https://www.allbusiness.com/rebuild-your-brand-after-pr-nightmare-18331-1.html

http://www.idc.com/prodserv/smartphone-market-share.jsp

http://fortune.com/2016/10/06/samsung-smartphone-recall-damage/

http://www.nytimes.com/2016/10/12/business/international/samsung-galaxy-note7-terminated.html?_r=0

CHAPTER 4:
WOMEN ARE EPIC COMPLAINERS?
https://academic.oup.com/jcr/article-abstract/10/1/73/1833503/An-Analysis-of-Consumer-Interaction-Styles-in-the

http://onlinelibrary.wiley.com/doi/10.1111/j.1745-6606.1975.tb00550.x/full

https://pjmedia.com/drhelen/2015/6/29/shocker-women-complain-more-and-men-just-eat-it-and-shut-up/

http://thinkingonthemargin.blogspot.com/2007/02/why-do-women-complain-more-than-men.html

http://www.businessnewsdaily.com/5601-gender-consumer-complaints.html

http://alycevayleauthor.com/2014/01/21/do-women-complain-more-than-men/

FACTS ABOUT FEMALE BUYING POWER
http://she-conomy.com/facts-on-women

http://www.dove.com/uk/stories/campaigns/real-beauty-sketches.html

http://www.artofmanliness.com/2011/08/16/manly-brand-icons/

MEN DIE SOONER THAN WOMEN
http://www.msn.com/en-us/health/wellness/11-reasons-men-die-sooner-than-women/ss-AA2gR0x

FEMALE BUYING POWER IN B2B SITUATIONS
https://www.atkearney.com/marketing-sales/ideas-insights/the-rise-of-the-female-economy-in-b2b

ANGRY CUSTOMERS WILL COME BACK
https://blog.kissmetrics.com/unhappy-customers-into-resource/

https://www.groovehq.com/support/how-to-handle-angry-customer-service-complaint-on-twitter

https://www.helpscout.net/blog/customer-complaints/

CHAPTER 5:
CUSTOMERS MIGHT BE CRAZY WITH THEIR MONEY

http://www.sjsu.edu/faculty/watkins/prospect.htm

https://en.wikipedia.org/wiki/Prospect_theory

http://authors.library.caltech.edu/22253/

http://faculty.som.yale.edu/nicholasbarberis/ptapp_final.pdf

HOW TO READ FACES – Jo-Ellan Dimitrius

http://dimita.com/dr-jo-ellan-dimitrius-has-been-dubbed-a-pre-trial-pro-by-the-american-bar-association/

SOCIAL LISTENING SOFTWARE

http://www.kana.com

http://keyhole.co/blog/the-top-25-social-media-monitoring-tools/

http://www.pcmag.com/roundup/342728/the-best-social-listening-and-influencer-identification-tool

CHAPTER 6
CUSTOMER JOURNEY MAPPING

https://www.maritzcx.com/lp/five-steps-to-uncovering-the-real-customer-experience-journey/?utm_source=bing&utm_medium=cpc&utm_campaign=tier%202&utm_content=customer-experience---journey-mapping&utm_term=customer%20journey%20mapping&utm_source=bing&utm_medium=cpc&utm_campaign=Tier%202&utm_term=customer%20journey%20mapping&utm_content=Customer%20Experience%20-%20Journey%20Mapping

http://www.cmswire.com/digital-experience/why-personas-matter-in-b2b-customer-journey-mapping/

http://customerthink.com/the-benefits-of-creating-a-customer-journey-map/

https://conversionxl.com/customer-journey-maps-better-website-retention/

MORE ON THE COMCAST COMEBACK http://www.timesfreepress.com/news/business/aroundregion/story/2015/oct/25/comcast-spends-300-million-adds-workers-improve-customer-service/332468/

http://nypost.com/2016/02/03/comcast-says-fixing-its-horrible-customer-service-is-paying-off/

http://motherboard.vice.com/read/comcast-investigating-customer-service-call-from-hell

THE CUSTOMER ISN'T SCORING THE COMPANY
http://lets.glance.net/blog/2015/03/scoring-the-customer-experience-nps-vs-csat-vs-ces

OTHER BOOKS
BY ROSS SHAFER

Nobody Moved Your Cheese
(How to Ignore the Experts and Trust Your Gut)

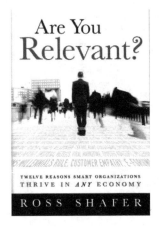

Are You Relevant?
(12 Reasons Smart Organizations Thrive in Any Economy)

The Customer Shouts Back
(How to Create Lifelong Customers)

Grab More Market Share
(How to Wrangle Business Away From Lazy Competitors)

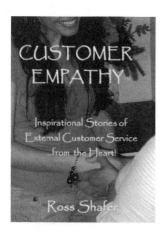

Customer Empathy
(Stories of Internal and External Customer Service)

Absolutely Necessary
(Bulletproof Tactics That Will Put You in High Demand)

Success: It's On You
(How to Accelerate the Outcomes you Want)

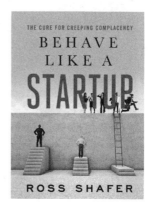

Behave Like a Startup
(The Cure for Creeping Complacency)

ABOUT ROSS SHAFER

Ross Shafer is a former network talk show host (*and believe it or not...a prominent stand up comedian*) who, for 25 years, has moonlighted as a relentless entrepreneur. His die-hard respect for customer buying habits led him to write and produce (14) HR training films and (9) business books on maximizing the customer experience, motivating the evolving workforce, and finding new revenue opportunities that are hiding in plain sight.

Aside from his touring schedule as a keynote speaker and consultant, Ross also writes and produces a weekly YouTube video blog called, the *Relevant Leader's Club*. He comments on issues that keep leaders up at night. He posts innovative ideas he's witnessed first hand. And, he interviews compelling thought leaders who can revolutionize the way you think about growing your business and career.

Ross lives with his wife Leah and their daughter Lauren in Colorado.

And yes, *that* is his real hair.

WAYS TO CONTACT
ROSS SHAFER

If you would like to talk to Ross about building a NO MORE CUSTOMER FRICTION PROGRAM for your company…or maybe you would like Ross to speak at your next meeting… please go to: https://RossShafer.com

phone: (910) 256-3495

email: Helen@RossShafer.com

Ross's video blog channel:
https://www.YouTube.com?user/RossShafer

twitter: @RossShafer

facebook: https://www.facebook.com/
RossShaferConsultants/

YOUR NOTES

YOUR NOTES

YOUR NOTES

YOUR NOTES